THE YOUNG OXFORD LIBRARY OF SCIENCE

Plants and Animals

Barbara Taylor

OXFORD
UNIVERSITY PRESS

OXFORD
UNIVERSITY PRESS

Great Clarendon Street, Oxford OX2 6DP

Oxford University Press is a department of the University of Oxford.
It furthers the University's objective of excellence in research, scholarship,
and education by publishing worldwide in

Oxford New York

Auckland Bangkok Buenos Aires Cape Town Chennai
Dar es Salaam Delhi Hong Kong Istanbul Karachi
Kolkata Kuala Lumpur Madrid Melbourne Mexico City Mumbai
Nairobi São Paulo Shanghai Singapore Taipei Tokyo Toronto

with an associated company in Berlin

Oxford is a registered trade mark of Oxford University Press
in the UK and in certain other countries

British Library Cataloguing in Publication Data available

Hardback ISBN 0-19-910934-6
Paperback ISBN 0-19-910935-4

1 3 5 7 9 10 8 6 4 2

Designed and typeset by Full Steam Ahead
Printed in Malaysia.

CONTENTS

LIFE ON EARTH

Imagine travelling back in time 4000 million years. You would find a very different Earth, with no plants, no animals, no bacteria, no viruses. No life at all. Only the crackling electricity of lightning storms, the intense heat and fumes of volcanic eruptions and the boom of meteorites hitting the Earth. There would be no oxygen for you to breathe and nothing to shield you from the Sun's powerful radiation. Yet somehow, in this hostile environment, the first incredible spark of life began.

No one knows for sure how this happened, but scientists think that energy from sunlight and lightning strikes triggered the formation of chemicals that could copy themselves. This may have taken place in the chemical 'soup' that existed in the oceans, in shallow pools or around volcanoes. The next crucial step was when the self-copying chemicals became trapped in 'bubbles' of oil, which held them together. These tiny blobs of chemicals were the beginnings of the first living cells.

mya = millions of years ago

CRETACEOUS

many turtles and crocodiles

250 mya
great extinction kills more than half of all living things

TRIAS
firs
dinosa

earliest snakes

modern bony fishe

PERMIAN

early sea-reptiles

290 mya

412 mya

insects invade land

DEVONIAN

early ferns

SILURIAN

first reptiles

first amphibi

435 mya

jawed fishes

winged insects

first ammonites (shellfishes)

ORDOVICIAN

first land plants

early jellyfishes

550 mya
explosion of new life forms

CARBONIFEROUS

jawless fishes

first trilobites

500 mya

CAMBRIAN

first bacteria
(3500 mya)

Earth forms
(4600 mya)

▲ Timeline of the history of life on Earth. The colours represent geological periods, some of which ended with mass extinctions of living creatures. If we imagine the whole history of the Earth happening in just 12 hours, then simple bacteria would appear after 3 hours, at 3 o'clock. The first worms and jellyfishes would clock in at about 10 o'clock, with the first dinosaurs appearing at 11.45. Humans would not appear until about a minute before 12 o'clock.

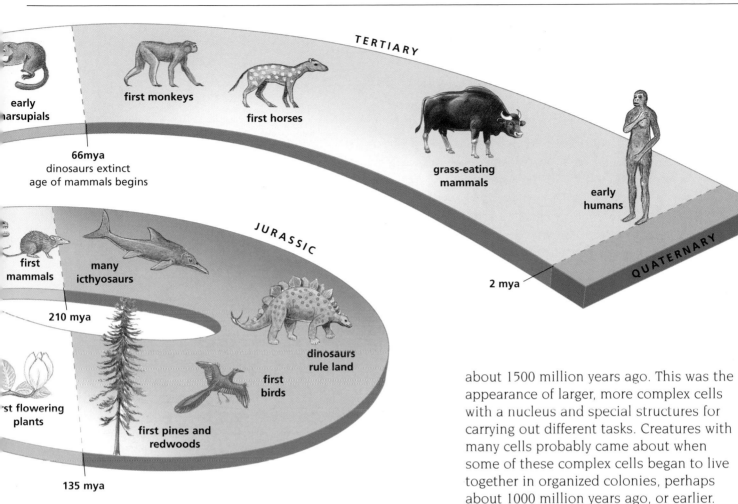

early marsupials

first monkeys

first horses

TERTIARY

grass-eating mammals

early humans

66mya
dinosaurs extinct
age of mammals begins

JURASSIC

first mammals

many icthyosaurs

210 mya

QUATERNARY

2 mya

dinosaurs rule land

first birds

first pines and redwoods

first flowering plants

135 mya

360 mya

What is life?

From the very first simple cells that lived on the Earth to the complex trees and tigers of today, all living things have certain things in common. They reproduce by making copies of themselves, they feed, they get energy from their food, they get rid of wastes and they respond to the world around them.

The first life forms

For almost 2000 million years after life began on the Earth, the only forms of life were microscopic, one-celled creatures similar to the bacteria of today. Some of them eventually began to use light from the Sun to make food, giving off oxygen in the process. As the oxygen built up in the atmosphere, it shielded the Earth from some of the Sun's harmful radiation.

Changing cells

The extra oxygen triggered the next milestone in the development of life,

about 1500 million years ago. This was the appearance of larger, more complex cells with a nucleus and special structures for carrying out different tasks. Creatures with many cells probably came about when some of these complex cells began to live together in organized colonies, perhaps about 1000 million years ago, or earlier.

Animal explosion

Around 600 million years ago, life really took off. There was a huge explosion of animal life in the oceans, and the ancestors of probably all the modern animal groups we know today came into being. Over hundreds of millions of years, some simple animals without backbones, which looked like jellyfishes or worms, developed into animals with backbones, including the first fishes.

Life on land

Another great landmark in the development of life happened about 400 million years ago, when life moved on to the land. Plants were first to make the move, followed by insects and other small animals, and finally 'walking fishes' called amphibians. From amphibians developed the first large land animals, the reptiles – such as the dinosaurs – and later birds and mammals, including humans.

key words

- bacteria
- cells
- colonies
- oxygen

CHANGE AND SURVIVAL

It is hard to believe that dogs such as wolfhounds and dachshunds are related. Yet people have developed over 100 breeds of dog from just one dog – the wolf – simply by choosing which dogs to breed together. This has been possible because of the huge amount of doggy variation that is hidden inside wolves.

If just one type of animal has so much hidden variation, think how much more there must be in the many millions of living things on the planet. Why are there so many different kinds of animal and plant, and why are they so good at what they do – flying, swimming, producing flowers, and so on? One of the main reasons is evolution. Variety is the raw material of evolution – the development of different forms of life over long periods of time.

4
Present day
Modern African elephants usually have two long tusks, a very long trunk and a large body.

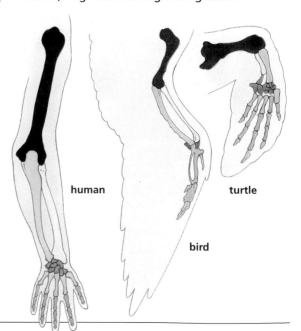

Natural selection

In the middle of the 19th century, Charles Darwin and Alfred Russel Wallace suggested that evolution happened because nature selected which variations would survive. As the environment changes over time, those individuals with variations that make them best suited to the environment are more likely to survive and reproduce, while other individuals die out. So as the environment changes, the individuals change too. This idea is called natural selection or 'the survival of the fittest'.

1
50 million years ago
Moeritherium had a flexible snout and long incisor teeth that jutted forwards.

2
35 million years ago
Phiomia was larger than *Moeritherium* and had a short trunk, a long lower jaw and four short tusks.

3
20 million years ago
Platybelodon was bigger than *Phiomia*, with a longer trunk and wide, spade-like teeth to scoop up plants.

3a
Deinotherium had large tusks which curved backwards. It was almost as big as modern elephants but became extinct about 2 million years ago.

▲ The first elephants were pig-sized animals with small tusks and no trunk. Over tens of millions of years, elephants evolved, finding better ways to survive, and to get their food. They changed into larger species, with long trunks, huge tusks and grinding teeth.

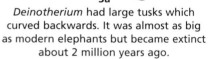

▶ Animals with backbones all have the same limb bones, which suggests that they evolved from the same ancestor. This illustration shows how the same set of bones has evolved to support flippers in turtles, wings in birds and arms in humans.

human

turtle

bird

DARWIN'S FINCHES

Charles Darwin found some of the most important evidence for his theory of evolution when he visited the Galapagos Islands in 1835. He suggested that the many different kinds, or species, of finch on the islands had all evolved from one species that somehow managed to reach the islands from mainland South America, some 1000 kilometres away. Over a long period of time, this one finch ancestor then evolved into 13 different species to take advantage of the different types of food and living space available on these isolated islands.

New life for old

Since life first appeared on Earth, millions of living things have died out (become extinct). They have been killed off by competition from other life forms, rapid changes in climate or changes caused by the drifting of continents about the globe. So the millions of different living things on Earth today are only a tiny fraction of all the living things that have ever existed.

Some extinctions happened gradually, but others were more sudden, and affected large numbers of living things. One of these mass extinctions took place about 65 million years ago, and wiped out the dinosaurs. It may have been caused by a large volcano exploding, or a meteorite hitting the Earth and throwing up clouds of dust that blocked out the Sun.

Evidence for evolution

Evidence for evolution comes partly from preserved remains of plants and animals that lived in the past, called fossils. These can be dated and some show the path that evolution has taken, for instance how

dolphin

icthyosaur

amphibians evolved from fishes or how birds evolved from reptiles. A few fossils record a sequence of changes over time, as with elephants or horses. There are many gaps in the fossil record however, since only one per cent of all life has been preserved as fossils.

Plants and animals alive today also provide evidence for evolution. Comparing the genes of both living and fossil creatures has helped scientists to work out which species have similar genes and so may be related to each other.

key words

- Darwin
- evolution
- extinctions
- fossils
- genes
- natural selection
- species
- variation

▲ Animals that look similar, such as modern dolphins and extinct ichthyosaurs, are not always related to each other. They may look the same because they have independently evolved to suit the same environment and way of life. This is called convergent evolution.

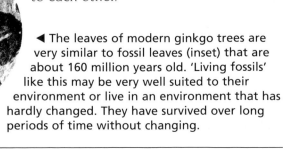

◄ The leaves of modern ginkgo trees are very similar to fossil leaves (inset) that are about 160 million years old. 'Living fossils' like this may be very well suited to their environment or live in an environment that has hardly changed. They have survived over long periods of time without changing.

GROUPING LIVING THINGS

Gorillas, chimpanzees and orang-utans are closely related to humans. Our blood is so similar that we could get a transfusion from a chimpanzee. We suffer from the same diseases. Even the brain cases of humans and gorillas are the same size at birth. So we are put together with them in the same group, called hominoids.

HOW A TIGER IS CLASSIFIED

GROUP	SUBDIVISION	MEANING
Kingdom	Animalia (animals)	
Phylum	Chordata	Nerve cord down back
Sub-phylum	Vertebrata (vertebrates)	Having a backbone
Class	Mammalia (mammals)	Animal with fur or hair, feeds on mother's milk
Order	Carnivora (carnivores)	Meat-eating
Family	Felidae	Cats
Genus	*Panthera*	Big cats
Species	*Panthera tigris*	Tiger

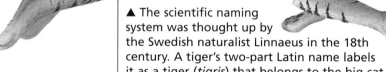

▲ The scientific naming system was thought up by the Swedish naturalist Linnaeus in the 18th century. A tiger's two-part Latin name labels it as a tiger (*tigris*) that belongs to the big cat group (*Panthera*).

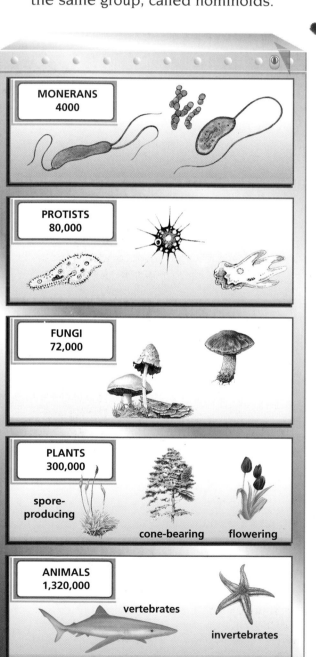

MONERANS
4000

PROTISTS
80,000

FUNGI
72,000

PLANTS
300,000
spore-producing
cone-bearing   flowering

ANIMALS
1,320,000
vertebrates
invertebrates

🔵 **key words**

- DNA
- kingdoms
- Linnaeus
- species

◀ Today, the living world is usually classified into five kingdoms – animals, plants, fungi, monerans (such as bacteria) and protists (such as algae and diatoms). The number beneath the name of each kingdom indicates the approximate number of species (kinds of creature) in each group. These are just the ones we know about – there are many millions more waiting to be discovered.

Classification is like a filing system. It is a way of organizing and making sense of the millions of kinds of living thing with which we share this planet. It is also often used as a way of understanding evolution.

Classification is about putting living things into groups that share certain features. The animal kingdom contains millions of different kinds, or species, of living thing. The smallest groups contain just one species.

A species is a collection of similar living things. In those living things that have males and females, members of a species can breed together.

Common features

Scientists once classified living things mainly by their shape and appearance and the way they develop. Now they can also compare the DNA (the chemical that makes up the genes) that parents pass on to their offspring. Living things that look the same (such as barnacles and limpets) may have very different DNA, which shows that they are not closely related.

MICROSCOPIC LIFE

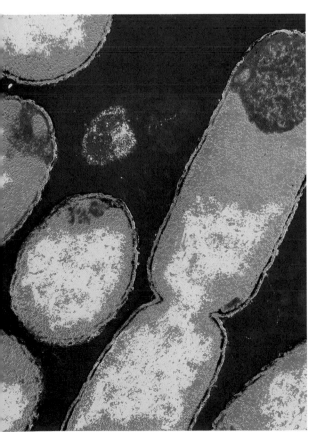

Your body is carrying over 100,000 billion hitchhikers. They are bacteria, the most abundant life forms on Earth. The bacteria that live on you are just a tiny fraction of the millions of different kinds of bacteria that exist.

Bacteria can only be seen with a very powerful microscope. A typical bacterial cell is about 1000 times smaller than an animal cell. Viruses are even smaller, and are not made up of cells. These tiny packages of genetic material are not true living things because they cannot grow and reproduce on their own. They come to life inside living cells, and some of them cause diseases such as the common cold, measles and Aids. They have to invade other cells in order to make copies of themselves.

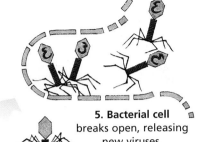

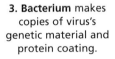

1. Virus lands on cell wall of bacterium.

2. Tail of virus injects genetic material into bacterium.

3. Bacterium makes copies of virus's genetic material and protein coating.

4. Parts of new viruses come together.

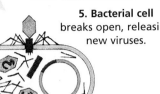

5. Bacterial cell breaks open, releasing new viruses.

Inside bacteria

Most bacteria consist of just one microscopic cell, without a control centre, or nucleus. Instead, bacteria have just a single loop of genetic instructions, or DNA.
   Most bacteria have rigid cell walls with a slimy outer covering. The cell walls are usually covered with tiny hairs. There are also larger strands called flagella, which help the bacteria to move.

Helpful and harmful bacteria

Most bacteria are harmless or even useful – sometimes extremely so. People use bacteria to make yoghurt and cheese, and some bacteria are used to 'grow' proteins such as insulin, which is used to treat diabetes. Bacteria play a vital role in breaking down natural wastes. But other bacteria, sometimes called germs, cause diseases such as cholera, tetanus and typhoid.

◄ Dividing *Bacillus* bacterium. A bacterium can divide into two once every 30 minutes, producing (in theory) 8 million new bacteria in a day. Fortunately, the numbers of bacteria are limited by the available food and space.

▲ Viruses called bacteriophages invade the cells of bacteria. They 'hijack' the cell's chemical processes, so that, instead of working normally, the cell makes copies of the virus.

In theory, one bacterium could produce nearly 5000 billion billion offspring in 24 hours.

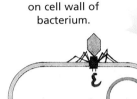

● key words
- bacteriophage
- cells
- DNA
- flagella
- germs
- virus

MUSHROOMS AND MOULDS

The mushrooms we eat and the mould that makes the drug penicillin are different kinds of tiny organisms called fungi. Fungi are found in every kind of environment – some can even live on petrol or plastic. For most of the time, fungi exist as nothing more than microscopic cells or a mass of branching threads. We only notice them when their reproductive structures, mushrooms or toadstools, burst out of the ground.

Fungi are neither plants nor animals – they are classified in their own separate kingdom. The cells of fungi divide in a completely different way from those of other living things. The cell walls of fungi are made of chitin, the material from which insects make their hard outer skeletons. Unlike green plants, fungi cannot use the Sun's energy to make food. Instead they absorb their food from other living things, or the dead remains of living things.

▶ This photograph, taken with a very powerful microscope, shows *Penicillium*, from which penicillin is made, growing on bread.

 key words

- fungi
- mould
- penicillin
- spores

Useful fungi

Fungi play a vital role in the natural world because they break down dead and decaying materials so that they can be recycled. They are a vital ingredient in the formation of soil. They are also useful to people in making bread, wine, beer and drugs such as penicillin. But fungal infections also destroy crops and cause diseases such as athlete's foot or ringworm.

2. Some of the hyphae join together to form a button-shaped fruiting body – the toadstool.

1. A spore germinates to form a network of branching threads called a mycelium. Each thread is called a hypha (plural hyphae).

3. This cross-section shows how the red cap expands into an umbrella shape.

5. The toadstool quickly decays.

4. Ripe spores drop from vertical flaps called gills under the cap and are blown away by the wind.

◀ New fungi grow from microscopic spores, which spread the fungus to new areas with the help of the wind, rain or insects. This diagram shows the life cycle of the fly agaric toadstool. One toadstool can produce as many as ten thousand million spores.

THE PLANT KINGDOM

A fly spots some sugary sap on a leaf and buzzes down for a snack. But it turns out to be a terrible mistake. The fly touches tiny trigger hairs on the surface of the leaf, which snaps shut in a fraction of a second. Trapped in its leafy prison, the fly is dissolved and turned into a soupy meal for the well-named 'Venus fly trap'.

Most plants cannot move as quickly as the Venus fly trap. Plants react much more slowly than animals do to changes in their surroundings. But in many ways, plants are more successful than animals. They have lived on the Earth for longer, and were the first living things to move out of the oceans onto the land. And without plants, all animals, including humans, would die.

Food factories

Plants can make their own food, but animals cannot. Animals either eat plants or other animals – which themselves live off plants.

The process plants use to make their food is photosynthesis. During photosynthesis, plants use the energy in sunlight to turn carbon dioxide gas from the air and water from the soil into food. They use a green chemical called chlorophyll to trap the Sun's energy, which is why most plants are green.

▶ The giant sequoia or redwood trees of California, USA, are among the biggest living things on Earth. The tallest one is over 112 m – as high as the American Statue of Liberty. The heaviest weighs as much as 4800 average-sized cars!

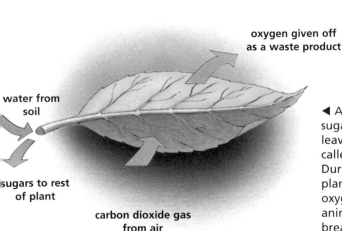

oxygen given off as a waste product

water from soil

sugars to rest of plant

carbon dioxide gas from air

◀ A plant makes sugary food inside its leaves in a process called photosynthesis. During photosynthesis, plants also produce oxygen gas, which all animals need to breathe to stay alive.

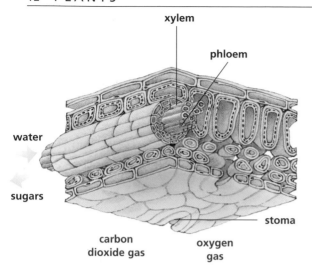

◀ A cross-section through a leaf. Tiny holes called stomata allow gases to pass in and out. Running through the roots, stems and leaves are two kinds of tube. The xylem carries water and minerals and the phloem carries food.

▶ Plants are divided into four main groups according to how they reproduce.

Mosses and liverworts
• live in damp places and produce spores
• most have no roots and no tubes inside them
• about 16,000 different kinds

Ferns
• live in damp places, especially rainforests, and produce spores
• have rigid stalks containing tubes, leaves called fronds and fine roots
• about 10,000 kinds of ferns, horsetails and clubmosses

Plant structure

A typical plant has roots to anchor it in the ground. The roots take up water and minerals from the soil. A stem or trunk links the roots to the leaves and holds them up so that they can collect sunshine and air for photosynthesis and breathing.

Plant groups

Scientists have identified more than 270,000 different kinds, or species, of plant. They are divided into four main groups according to how they reproduce: mosses and liverworts; ferns; conifers (plants with cones); and flowering plants. More than 80 per cent of all plants are flowering plants.

Spore plants

Ferns, horsetails, mosses and liverworts reproduce by means of spores. These dust-like particles are simpler than seeds and do not have a food store. They consist only of genetic material (DNA) inside a protective coat. Spore-producing plants appeared on Earth before flowering plants. They can only live and reproduce in damp places.

Seed plants

The purpose of a flower is to make seeds, which spread away from the parent plant and grow into new plants. Conifers also produce seeds, which develop on woody cones. A seed contains the tiny beginnings of a plant and a food store, all surrounded by a tough outer coat. Seeds can stay dormant ('asleep') for years before growing. This helps them to survive cold or drought.

▼ A fern spore grows into a tiny, heart-shaped prothallus, which produces sperm and egg cells. A sperm has to swim through moisture on the surface of the prothallus to fuse with an egg cell before a new fern can develop.

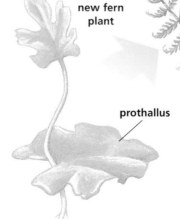

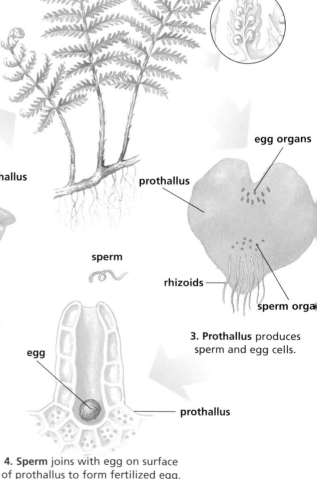

2. **Spore cases** form on fully grown ferns.

spore cases on underside of leaf

egg organs

rhizoids

sperm organs

3. **Prothallus** produces sperm and egg cells.

new fern plant

prothallus

prothallus

sperm

1. **New fern** plant grows from fertilized egg.

egg

prothallus

4. **Sperm** joins with egg on surface of prothallus to form fertilized egg.

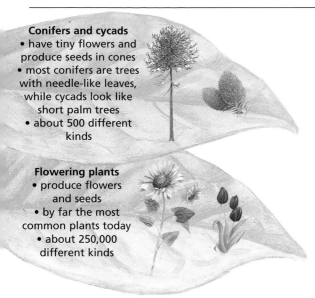

Conifers and cycads
• have tiny flowers and produce seeds in cones
• most conifers are trees with needle-like leaves, while cycads look like short palm trees
• about 500 different kinds

Flowering plants
• produce flowers and seeds
• by far the most common plants today
• about 250,000 different kinds

Plants with cones

A typical conifer produces separate male and female cones. The male cones produce pollen and the female cones produce egg cells. Ripe male cones open to release clouds of pollen, which are carried by the wind to female cones. There the pollen joins with (fertilizes) the egg cells. Seeds then develop within the female cone. The seeds of conifers are not completely enclosed within fruits, as are the seeds of flowering plants.

Flowering groups

The largest group of flowering plants is called the dicotyledons, or dicots for short. Most common flowers and vegetables are dicots, as are all broad-leaved trees such as oaks. The sprouting seeds of a dicot have two seed leaves – 'di' means two and cotyledon means seed leaf. Dicot leaves come in many shapes, with their veins forming a network through the leaf. The flower parts usually occur in multiples of four or five.

The oldest trees alive today are bristlecone pines. Some bristlecones started to grow in the White Mountains of California over 4600 years ago. These trees were in their prime when the first Pharaohs were ruling ancient Egypt. When Christ was born, they were already 2600 years old.

The other main group of flowering plants is called the monocotyledons, or monocots. Grasses, palms, lilies, orchids and tulips are all monocots. They have long, narrow leaves with parallel veins and flower parts that occur in multiples of three.

Plants with flowers

From grasses and apple trees to daffodils and orchids, flowering plants are a very varied group of plants. They evolved together with insects, and many flowers depend on insects to carry their pollen. The bright colours and scents of flowers, and the sugary nectar within them, attract animals (usually insects), which then carry away pollen on their bodies. Flowers that use the wind to carry their pollen, such as grasses, tend to be small, and dull.

key words

• cones
• egg cells
• photosynthesis
• pollen
• seeds
• spores

▼ In a flower, the male sex cells are in the pollen grains, which are held in sacs called anthers. Pollen lands on the female part of a flower, the stigma. The pollen grain grows a tubule down from the stigma to the ovary. There it fertilizes a female sex cell to make a seed.

stigma
style (stalk)
petal
anther (pollen sac)
filament (stalk)
stamen
pollen
ovule
female sex cell
stalk
first true leaf
young plant
cotyledon
ovary contains ovules with female sex cells
pollen grain
style (stalk)
stigma
pollen tube
stigma
ovary wall
food store
new plant ready to grow
seed
pollen fertilizes egg cell

THE ANIMAL KINGDOM

Even though it is small enough to fit into a jam jar, the blue-ringed octopus is one of the world's deadliest animals. Its poison glands are as large as its brain and one octopus contains enough poison to kill 10 people. The octopus normally uses its poison to catch the crabs it feeds on.

All animals have to eat plants or other animals instead of making their own food, and this is the main difference between animals and plants. The variety of ways in which animals catch their food is an important reason for the huge diversity in their shapes and sizes. Most animals need a gut in which to digest their food.

Animal characteristics

Animals need to be able to move around to find their food. Most use muscles that pull on some sort of rigid framework, usually an internal or external skeleton. They also have nerves to control their movement and senses to detect what is happening around them. Most animals have some form of 'brain' to control their nerves and senses, which is usually located in a head.

Keeping warm

The body temperature of most animals varies with that of their surroundings. This is called

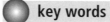

key words

- cold-blooded
- invertebrates
- nerves
- senses
- skeleton
- vertebrates
- warm-blooded

▼ A cheetah chasing a Thomson's gazelle. Cheetahs are the world's fastest land animals over short distances, and so they are excellent hunters. They can accelerate from 0 to 90 km/h in just three seconds and run at nearly 100 km/h. But they have to rest after about 20 seconds because they get too hot and run out of oxygen.

▲ Anemones are animals, although they look rather like flowering plants and they do not usually move around. Instead they use their petal-like tentacles to catch food, such as tiny fishes, which they stun with stinging cells on their tentacles.

being a 'cold-blooded' animal (although their blood can be warm or cold depending on the temperature around them). Cold-blooded animals are more common in warmer places.

Only two groups of animals, birds and mammals, can control their body temperature. This is called being warm-blooded and it means that the animal's body stays at the same high temperature, no matter how hot or cold it is around them. Warm-blooded animals can live in both warm and cold places. However, keeping their bodies warm all the time uses a lot of energy, so they must eat more often than cold-blooded animals.

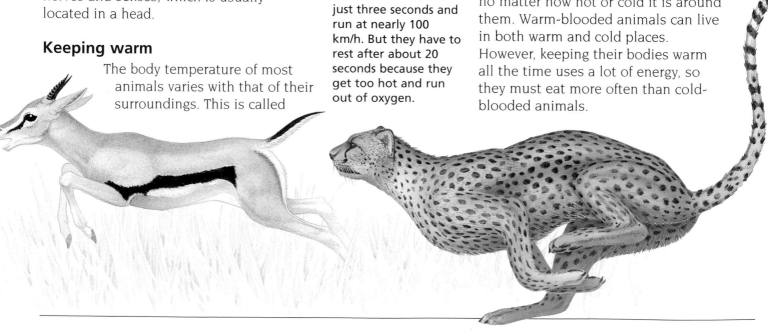

Invertebrates
About 33 different groups, including sponges, jellyfishes, worms, snails, insects and starfishes. Many live in water but some, such as insects, live on land. They are all cold-blooded.

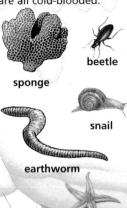
sponge

beetle

snail

earthworm

starfish

Fishes
Two main groups – fishes with a bony skeleton (most fishes) and fishes with a skeleton made of cartilage, such as sharks and rays. They live in water, have a scaly skin and are cold-blooded.

trout

stingray

Amphibians
Three main groups – salamanders and newts, frogs and toads, and blindworms (caecilians). They live partly in water and partly on land, have a smooth, moist skin and are cold-blooded.

newt

frog

Reptiles
Three main groups – turtles and tortoises, snakes and lizards, and crocodiles and alligators. Many live in warm places on land but some, such as turtles, live in water. They have scales and are cold-blooded.

lizard

tortoise

Birds
28–30 different groups, from sparrows and parrots to eagles and penguins. They live all over the world, have feathers and are warm-blooded.

finch

penguin

Mammals
21 different groups, from mice and bats to giraffes and bears. They live all over the world, have fur and are warm-blooded.

woodmouse

giraffe

Animal skeletons

Animals are sometimes divided into two groups, vertebrates and invertebrates. A vertebrate is an animal with a backbone, which is a column of segments or vertebrae supporting the central nerve cord. Its body is supported by a bony skeleton. Most of the bigger, more complicated and more familiar animals – including fishes, reptiles, birds and mammals – are vertebrates.

An invertebrate is an animal without a backbone or any bones. Over 90 per cent of all animals are invertebrates, including insects, snails and worms. The bodies of invertebrates may be supported by a hard shell or an outer skeleton, called an exoskeleton. But a jellyfish is supported only by the water around it, while worms are supported by the pressure of fluid-filled spaces inside their bodies.

▲ Animals can be divided into six major groups. About 1.5 million different species of animals have been identified so far, and over 1 million of these are insects. The five groups of vertebrates include only about 50,000 known species.

◄ Skeletons are especially important for animals that live on land.

The external skeleton of an invertebrate animal such as a scorpion is made of a hard, lightweight substance called chitin. An external skeleton cannot grow. It has to be shed, or moulted, to allow the animal to grow.

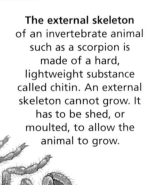

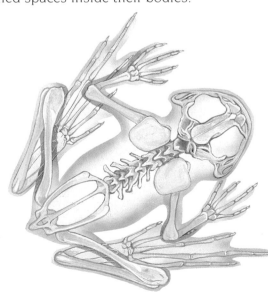

The internal skeleton of a vertebrate such as a frog supports its body and protects its soft internal organs, such as its heart. Muscles attached to the bones of the skeleton enable the animal to move. As the frog grows, its skeleton grows too.

BUILDING BLOCKS OF LIFE

What do you have in common with a tree, a worm and a crocodile? The answer is cells. Trees, worms, crocodiles, humans and all living things are made up of the same tiny building blocks, called cells. Some very simple living things are made of just one cell, but a tiny worm has about 1000 cells and an adult human being has about 10 million million cells.

Cells are usually far too small to see without a microscope, but they are remarkably complicated. They are like tiny chemical factories. Substances constantly stream in and out of cells. Chemical reactions happen in a carefully controlled way, and energy is released from food to fuel all of life's activities.

Most cells are microscopic, but the egg cell of an ostrich is 15–20 cm long, and some giraffe nerve cells reach more than 4 m long.

ROBERT HOOKE
The first person to draw the cells he saw under a microscope was the English scientist Robert Hooke (1635–1703). He built his own light microscope and drew pictures of the honeycomb of cells in cork in 1665. He even called them cells, although the importance of his work was not recognized for another 100 years. Hooke's studies of microscopic fossils led him to become one of the first people to put forward a theory of evolution.

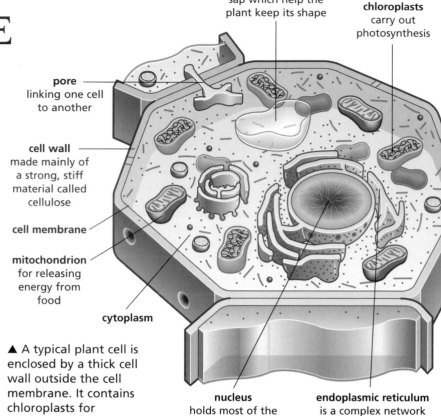

vacuoles large spaces filled with sap which help the plant keep its shape

chloroplasts carry out photosynthesis

pore linking one cell to another

cell wall made mainly of a strong, stiff material called cellulose

cell membrane

mitochondrion for releasing energy from food

cytoplasm

nucleus holds most of the cell's genetic material

endoplasmic reticulum is a complex network of membranes studded with ribosomes for making proteins

▲ A typical plant cell is enclosed by a thick cell wall outside the cell membrane. It contains chloroplasts for making food.

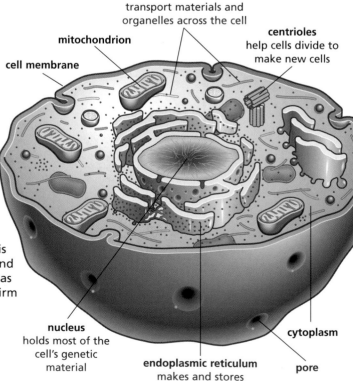

microtubules transport materials and organelles across the cell

mitochondrion

cell membrane

centrioles help cells divide to make new cells

▶ A typical animal cell is about 0.02 mm across. It has no chloroplasts or vacuoles and is surrounded by a thin cell membrane. This makes it soft and flexible, whereas a plant cell is firm and rigid.

nucleus holds most of the cell's genetic material

endoplasmic reticulum makes and stores proteins

cytoplasm

pore

Inside a cell

A cell is a bag full of jelly-like fluid called cytoplasm. Most cells have different structures, called organelles, within the cytoplasm.

The different organelles carry out different tasks, such as releasing energy from food, which is called respiration. Respiration takes place in sausage-shaped organelles called mitochondria. The cell is usually controlled by a nucleus, which contains the chemical instructions, or DNA, needed to make it work.

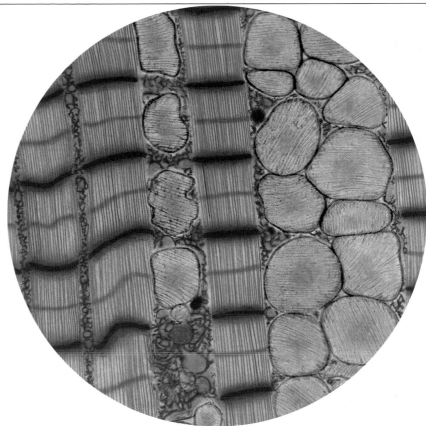

▶ A microscope picture of heart muscle. Muscle cells use a lot of energy, so the long, thin muscle cells are tightly packed with mitochondria, which are the cells' power stations.

Cell boundaries

To stay alive, all cells have to create a stable set of conditions inside that are different from those outside. To do this, they seal themselves off from their surroundings by means of a thin 'bag', or membrane. A cell membrane is so thin that a pile of 10,000 cell membranes, one on top of the other, would equal the thickness of this page. Cell membranes control the substances that pass in and out of the cells as well as detecting and responding to chemical signals from their environment and other cells.

Each organelle inside a cell is also surrounded by a membrane so that the different activities of a cell are separated and do not interfere with one another. The nucleus, mitocondria and chloroplasts have double membranes. The membranes inside a cell provide a large surface area on which chemical reactions can occur.

Simple cells

Bacteria have much smaller, simpler cells than other forms of life. Although they have rigid cell walls and membranes, they have no nucleus and no mitochondria. They have just a single loop of DNA, called the nucleoid, as well as food granules and ribosomes, which produce proteins.

Working together

In living things made of large numbers of cells, there are many different types of cell. A rabbit has more than 250 different cells; you have about 200. Groups of cells of the same type are packed together to form tissues, such as nerve tissue. In a complex plant or animal, separate tissues are joined together to form organs, such as leaves, flowers, lungs or eyes.

▼ A nerve cell, like these brain cells, has a special membrane that passes electrical signals along its length. The signals pass from one nerve cell to another across tiny gaps called synapses.

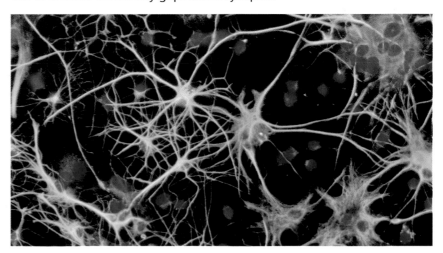

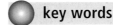
key words

- cells
- DNA
- Hooke
- membrane
- nucleus
- organelles

THE BLUEPRINT FOR LIFE

Why do mother cats always give birth to kittens? Why do poppy seeds always grow into poppy plants? And why do children take after their parents? The answer lies in their genes, sets of instructions about colour, shape and size, which are passed on from generation to generation. The study of genes is called genetics.

Inside every one of your cells is the same set of up to 100,000 separate genes. These genes add up to a three-billion-point blueprint for building you from scratch – your genome. Each of the cells in your body uses only a tiny fraction of its total set of chemical instructions, depending on the jobs it carries out. The rest of the genes in the cell are 'switched off'.

Where are genes?

Genes are in the nucleus, or control centre, of a cell. They are arranged along long, thin thread-like structures called chromosomes, rather like beads on a necklace. Different animals and plants have different numbers of chromosomes – humans have 46, most snakes have 36, horses have 63, while some ferns have 500 or more.

How genes work

Genes are made of a chemical called deoxyribonucleic acid, or DNA. DNA works by telling a cell how to make the proteins that keep the cell alive and growing. Small sections of the enormous DNA molecule carry the instructions for making individual proteins. The machinery for making these proteins is on structures called ribosomes, which are outside the nucleus. The DNA itself never leaves the nucleus. Instead, small sections are copied on to another chemical, called messenger RNA. This carries the instructions for making a particular protein to the ribosomes.

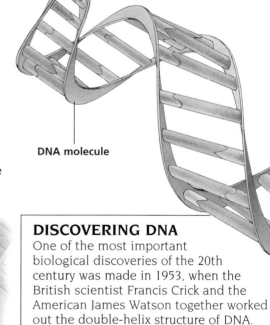

cell

chromosome pair

nucleus

chromosome

DNA molecule

▶ Each chromosome in the nucleus is an enormously long molecule of DNA, coiled and coiled again. This diagram shows how the double-stranded DNA copies itself, by splitting into two single strands and forming a new double strand on each half.

Nearly a third of a human being's genes are the same as the genes of a lettuce.

 key words

- chromosomes
- DNA
- genes
- genome
- meiosis
- mutation

DISCOVERING DNA

One of the most important biological discoveries of the 20th century was made in 1953, when the British scientist Francis Crick and the American James Watson together worked out the double-helix structure of DNA. They used information from X-ray photographs of crystals of DNA, taken by scientists Maurice Wilkins and Rosalind Franklin, to work out the DNA shape. DNA is shaped rather like a twisted ladder. This shape is called a double helix. The rungs of the ladder are made up of four chemical building blocks, adenine, guanine, thymine and cytosine. Like the letters of an alphabet, these building blocks can be arranged in different ways to make up the 'words' of the genes. So genetic instructions are in the form of a chemical code.

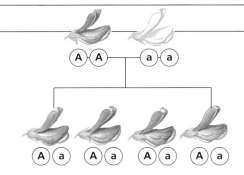

GREGOR MENDEL

A Czech monk called Gregor Mendel made the first important discoveries in genetics. 1865, Mendel was experimenting with pea plants. In one experiment, he bred together plants that had white flowers with ones that had purple flowers. Instead of getting some white and some purple flowers, he found that all the new plants had purple flowers.

To explain this, we have to remember that chromosomes come in pairs, so each plant has two genes for flower colour. What Mendel showed was that the gene for purple flowers

(**A** in the diagram) is dominant over the gene for white flowers (**a**). So if a plant has one purple-flower gene and one white-flower gene, the plant has purple flowers. The white flower gene is called recessive. It only shows if a plant has two white-flower genes.

KEY

adenine
always pairs
with thymine

thymine

guanine
always pairs
with cytosine

cytosine

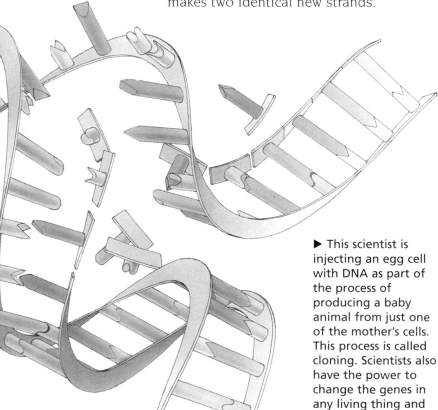

Copying genes

Every time a new cell is made, the DNA is copied so that each new cell has its own identical copy of all the genes. The structure of DNA makes the genes easy to copy. A DNA strand separates down the middle and spare chemical building blocks join up with their matching pairs on the separated strands. So one strand of DNA makes two identical new strands.

Changing genes

Genes can change if mistakes are made during the copying process, or if they are damaged by chemicals or radiation. They also change when they are mixed up during sexual reproduction. A permanent change to a piece of DNA is called a mutation. Most mutations are harmful, but a few produce helpful characteristics.

Genes and environment

The final appearance and behaviour of an individual is determined both by its genes and by outside influences. These influences include things like how much food it eats, what climate it lives in and whether it has suffered disease or injury during its development. But only those characteristics controlled by its genes can be inherited.

▶ This scientist is injecting an egg cell with DNA as part of the process of producing a baby animal from just one of the mother's cells. This process is called cloning. Scientists also have the power to change the genes in any living thing and introduce the genes from one species into another.

NEW GENERATIONS

Take a closer look at a rose bush on a hot summer's day and you may find it is covered with armies of greenfly. The reason there are so many greenfly is that they reproduce amazingly quickly. Female greenfly can give birth to identical female babies without mating with male greenfly. In just two weeks, one female and her daughters can have over 1300 babies.

Without reproduction, life on Earth would grind to a halt. Reproduction allows living things to replace themselves and increase their numbers. It also allows them to change, or evolve, over time. When they reproduce, living things pass on their genes – the chemical codes inside their cells that control their characteristics – to their offspring.

There are two forms of reproduction: asexual (non-sexual) reproduction and sexual reproduction.

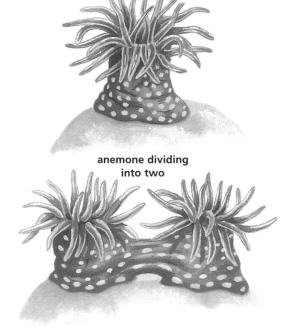

anemone dividing into two

▲ Anemones reproduce asexually. The anemone copies all its genes and then splits into two, making two genetically identical individuals. Living things made of one cell, such as bacteria and amoebas, also reproduce like this.

Asexual reproduction

Asexual reproduction is the simplest and quickest form of reproduction. The parent may just split into two or more pieces, or grow an extra part that becomes a new individual. Female eggs may also grow into babies without any input from the male, as happens in greenfly. In asexual reproduction offspring are identical to their parents.

key words

- asexual reproduction
- egg
- fertilization
- genes
- pollen
- sexual reproduction
- sperm

◀ Bees fly from flower to flower, feeding on nectar and pollen. As they do so, some pollen gets caught on the bee's body and is carried from the male parts of one flower to the female parts of another flower. This is called pollination.

After 7 months, one pair of cockroaches could have 164,000 million descendants.

Sexual reproduction

Sexual reproduction involves the joining together of two special sex cells, one from each parent. In animals, the male parent produces sperm cells and the female parent produces egg cells. In plants with flowers or cones, the male cells are called pollen and the female cells are called egg cells. To produce a new individual, a sperm cell or a pollen cell must join with an egg cell. This joining together is called fertilization.

Sexual reproduction mixes up the genes twice – once when the sex cells are made and once when fertilization happens. So each individual offspring is different from its parents and from its brothers and sisters.

Fertilization

In flowering plants the pollen and egg cells often come from different plants. The egg cells stay put but the pollen travels from one flower to another with the help of the wind, water or animals. This is called cross-fertilization. Pollen may also sometimes fertilize flowers on the same plant. This is called self-fertilization.

In most animals that live in the water, such as fishes, fertilization happens outside the animals' bodies. The eggs and sperm are shed into the water and fertilization happens there. Animals that live on land

▶ Some frogs make a foam nest to protect their eggs but then go away and leave them alone. Animals that do not care for their eggs or young usually produce large numbers of them. Many will die, but a few will survive to pass their genes on to the next generation.

usually fertilize the eggs inside the female's body because eggs and sperm quickly dry out and die in the open air.

Why sex is useful

Sexual reproduction is more complicated than asexual reproduction, but it does have one important advantage. The offspring are different from their parents and from each other, and stand a better chance of surviving, especially if conditions change.

▼ In sexual reproduction, there are two parents, and the offspring receive half their genes from the male parent and half from the female parent. The genes are mixed up so that each offspring has a different set of genes.

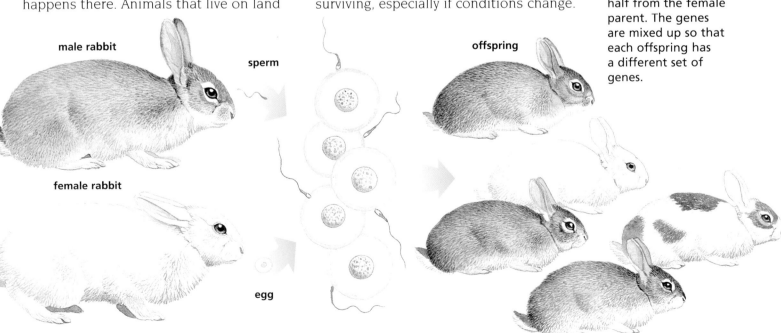

male rabbit

sperm

female rabbit

egg

offspring

SENSING THE SURROUNDINGS

Piercing the blackness of an African night comes the strange, child-like cry of a bushbaby. Its sensitive ears pick up the faint sounds of insects moving through the trees, while its enormous eyes focus on its prey in the moonlight. Keeping its feet clamped firmly to the branch, the bushbaby suddenly shoots out its body and hands to grab an insect meal out of the darkness.

Unlike bushbabies, we are creatures of the daytime and rely heavily our sense of sight – on detecting the light bouncing off things around us. It is hard for us to imagine what life must be like for animals that live in a world dominated by other signals, such as smells, sounds, heat or even electricity. We are totally unaware of millions of the smells that dogs can sense and are only able to hear about one third of the sounds that elephants make.

▶ Many bats use their own radar system – called echolocation – to detect flying insects at night. They make high-pitched clicking sounds and use their huge ears to pick up the echoes bouncing back from their prey.

Sight

Nearly all animals have organs that can sense the difference between light and dark. Most animals have eyes, which give them a picture of their surroundings.

Insects have compound eyes, which are made up of hundreds of tiny lenses packed closely together. All mammals have eyes similar to human eyes, containing a single lens. Nocturnal animals, which come out at night, have big eyes to let in as much light as possible. They often have a special layer in the eye that reflects light. This is what makes a cat's eyes shine in the dark.

◀ A fruit fly does not see the world in quite the same way as we do. Its compound eyes have many separate lenses and probably give a blurred picture of its surroundings. But they are good at detecting movement.

Hearing

Most animals pick up sounds with ears in their heads. Animals that rely on their hearing to hunt prey have particularly large ears. The desert fox is an example. Animals that live in water have ears too. Whales, for example, have good hearing and can pick up the sound of other whales singing many kilometres away.

Other animals sense sounds using different parts of their bodies. Among insects, earwigs pick up sounds through the hairs on their pincers, mosquitoes use antennae, and crickets have ears on their legs.

▲ The woodmouse uses its long, sensitive whiskers to feel its way through tangled undergrowth and narrow spaces.

Smell and taste

The sense of taste is closely linked with the sense of smell. These two senses allow animals to find food, send smelly messages to one another and avoid things that are harmful. Mammals have a nose for smelling things, but snakes smell with their tongue and moths with their antennae. Many animals use their tongues for tasting things, but octopuses taste with their tentacles and flies taste with their feet.

Special senses

Scientists have only recently begun to discover more about the special senses that certain animals possess that are completely outside human experience. Some animals can detect electricity, magnetism, water vibrations and heat. Birds use their magnetic sense to help them find their way when they migrate.

Most fishes have special lateral lines along the sides of their bodies which help them to pick up vibrations in the water. Sharks can also pick up electrical signals from the muscles of fishes to help them zoom in on their prey with deadly accuracy.

▼ Pit vipers have special heat holes on the side of the face, which pick up the heat given off by warm-blooded prey, such as mice. This helps these snakes to detect their prey in total darkness.

▲ The feathery antennae of the male moon moth have many branches on which the moth can pick up scent particles from the air. A male moth can detect the scent of a female moth from several kilometres away.

 key words

- echolocation
- hearing
- senses
- sight
- smell
- taste

ANIMAL HABITS

A young chimpanzee watches closely as its mother breaks off a strong, bendy plant stem and pulls off the leaves. Then she pushes the stem inside a termite mound and pulls out a juicy termite snack. It will take the young chimp many years to learn how to do this properly.

▲ In a wolf pack, each wolf knows its place. High-ranking (dominant) wolves stand tall, with their tail and ears up. Low-ranking or submissive wolves lie on their back to show that they will not fight.

Almost anything an animal does is a form of behaviour. Chimpanzees digging for termites, cranes leaping into the air in a courtship dance, lion cubs playing, wasps building a nest – all these are examples of animal behaviour. Many of the most interesting types of behaviour happen within a species as individuals defend a territory, find a mate, help each other to hunt, drive enemies away or raise young.

Learned or in-built?

A young chimp can learn how to 'fish' for termites because it has inherited the ability and intelligence to carry out this type of behaviour from its mother. There are two main types of behaviour – instinctive or innate behaviour, which is handed on from generation to generation; and learned behaviour, which an animal learns during its lifetime. An animal's behaviour is often a complex mixture of instinctive and learned behaviour.

Animals are born with the ability to behave in certain fixed or automatic ways. Some animals rely almost entirely on this automatic behaviour. Insect behaviour is largely automatic, for instance, and spiders do not have to learn how to spin a web. Fixed or instinctive behaviour is controlled by an animal's genes. If the environment changes, those animals that are best suited to the new conditions are more likely to survive to reproduce, and so pass on their genes to the next generation. Learned behaviour, on the other hand, is not passed on from one generation to the next.

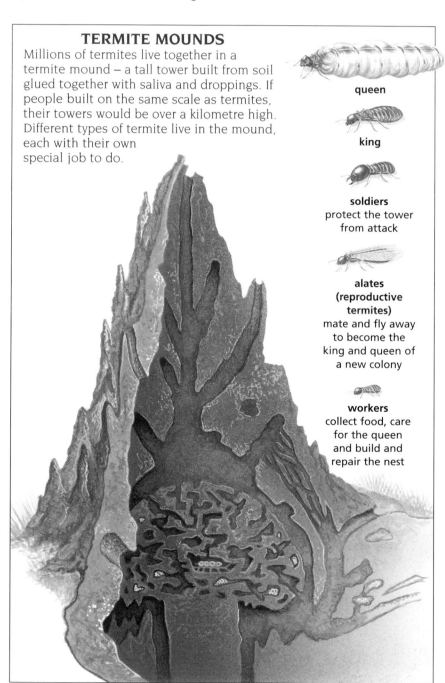

TERMITE MOUNDS

Millions of termites live together in a termite mound – a tall tower built from soil glued together with saliva and droppings. If people built on the same scale as termites, their towers would be over a kilometre high. Different types of termite live in the mound, each with their own special job to do.

queen

king

soldiers
protect the tower from attack

alates (reproductive termites)
mate and fly away to become the king and queen of a new colony

workers
collect food, care for the queen and build and repair the nest

▶ Male bighorn sheep fight to decide which are the strongest and most dominant individuals. Their fights are head-butting contests, which involve tremendous clashes of horns.

key words

- aestivation
- hibernation
- imprinting
- instinctive behaviour
- learned behaviour
- migration

Communication

The way an animal behaves is influenced by the way it interacts or communicates with other members of its own species. Although animals cannot talk, they can send each other messages using sounds, scents or body language, such as facial expressions. Female fireflies even use patterns of flashing lights to attract a mate.

Surviving the seasons

Different patterns of behaviour may help animals to survive seasonal changes in the weather. Many birds and some mammals, fishes and insects migrate – they make long journeys to avoid bad weather and poor food supplies, or to find a safer place to give birth to their young.

Other animals survive very cold weather or very dry weather by going into a deep sleep. Surviving cold conditions like this is called hibernation. Sleeping through hot, dry conditions is called aestivation.

KONRAD LORENZ

Konrad Lorenz (1903–1989) was one of the first scientists to study animal behaviour. He noticed that there is a period of intense learning during the first few hours of an animal's life, called imprinting, in which it learns to recognize its parents and its species. Some young geese treated Lorenz as their 'mother' because he was the first large object they saw when they hatched.

▶ Monarch butterflies migrate from Canada to Mexico for the winter, a journey of some 4000 kilometres. Among the Mexican pine trees, the butterflies hibernate in enormous clusters so that the trees seem to be dripping with butterflies.

ANIMALS WITHOUT BACKBONES

A cloud of black ink suddenly spreads through the sea water. It forms a 'smoke screen' that hides a squid as it darts quickly away from danger. Squid are the fastest swimming invertebrates, or animals without backbones.

Squid are also the largest invertebrates – giant squid can grow up to 18 metres long. But most invertebrates are small animals. It is only in the sea, where the water provides support, that they can grow into giants.

Invertebrate groups

Invertebrates are an incredibly diverse collection of animals. Ninety-nine per cent of all animals are invertebrates. They live all over the world – in the sea, in fresh water and on land. There are probably between 3 and 15 million kinds, or species, although only about a million species have been identified. They include sponges, worms, starfishes, snails, insects and crabs.

▶ Corals have a hard skeleton that supports and protects the soft living coral. Millions of coral skeletons build up to form coral reefs.

key words

- backbone
- invertebrates
- skeleton

Skeleton on the outside

Many invertebrate groups have hard external skeletons. These provide a strong, rigid surface to which muscles can be attached. Invertebrate skeletons are often divided into segments, allowing the animal to twist, turn and squirm along more easily.

▼ Molluscs are the second largest group of invertebrates after arthropods (see next page).

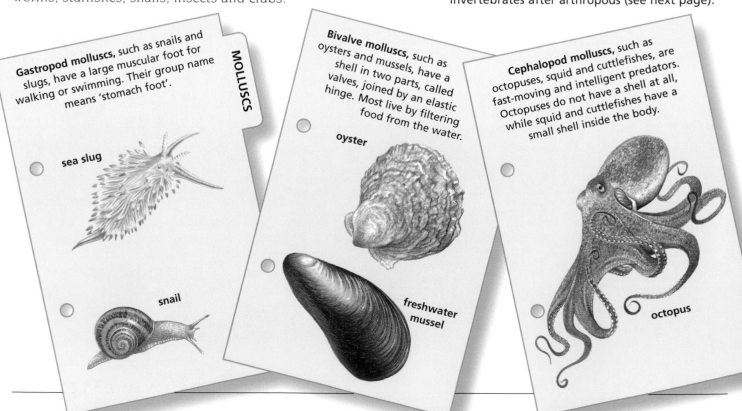

Gastropod molluscs, such as snails and slugs, have a large muscular foot for walking or swimming. Their group name means 'stomach foot'.

MOLLUSCS

sea slug

snail

Bivalve molluscs, such as oysters and mussels, have a shell in two parts, called valves, joined by an elastic hinge. Most live by filtering food from the water.

oyster

freshwater mussel

Cephalopod molluscs, such as octopuses, squid and cuttlefishes, are fast-moving and intelligent predators. Octopuses do not have a shell at all, while squid and cuttlefishes have a small shell inside the body.

octopus

A major advantage of the external skeleton is that it acts as a suit of protective armour. The shell of a snail, or the hard wing cases of a beetle, help to protect the soft body of the animal inside them.

Spiny skins

Starfishes and sea urchins are part of a big group of invertebrates called echinoderms, which means 'spiny-skinned'. Unlike any other animals, they have skeletons made of hard plates just beneath the skin. Most also have lots of small tube-feet with suckers on the end.

The bodies of many echinoderm's have no front or back. Instead, they are based on a circular plan. Often an echinoderm's body is made up of five symmetrical parts, arranged like the spokes of a wheel.

▶ The body of a jellyfish is 95 per cent water. It does not have a skeleton and is supported entirely by the sea water it lives in. A jellyfish uses the stings on its tentacles to defend itself from predators and catch food. The stings are armed with spines like miniature harpoons and are often loaded with poison.

▼ More than 75 per cent of all animals are arthropods. All arthropods have jointed bodies protected by a tough outer case.

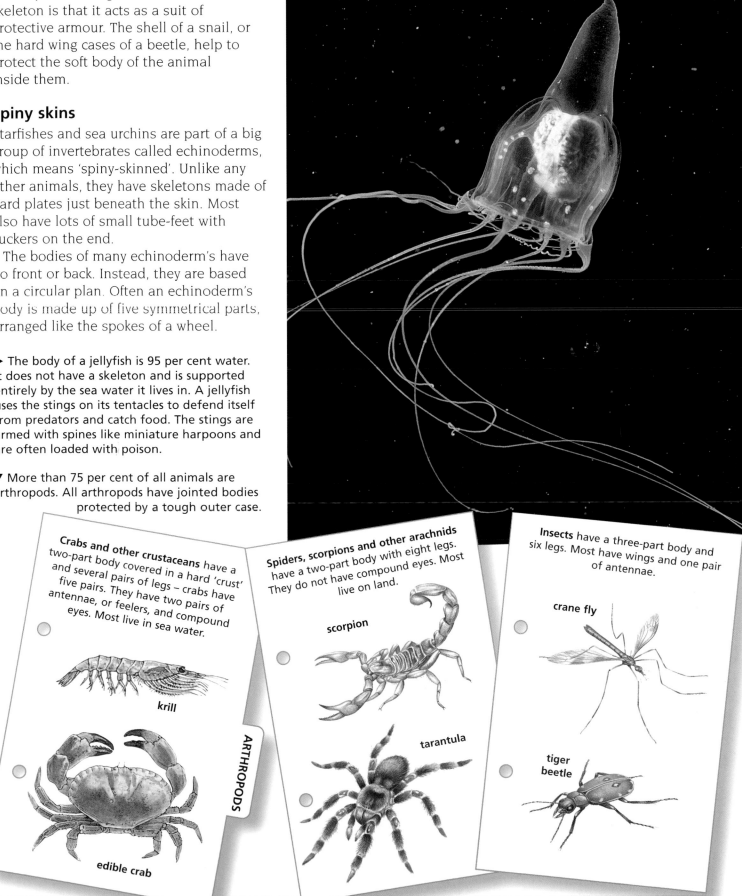

Crabs and other crustaceans have a two-part body covered in a hard 'crust' and several pairs of legs – crabs have five pairs. They have two pairs of antennae, or feelers, and compound eyes. Most live in sea water.

krill

edible crab

ARTHROPODS

Spiders, scorpions and other arachnids have a two-part body with eight legs. Most They do not have compound eyes. Most live on land.

scorpion

tarantula

Insects have a three-part body and six legs. Most have wings and one pair of antennae.

crane fly

tiger beetle

SIX-LEGGED WONDERS

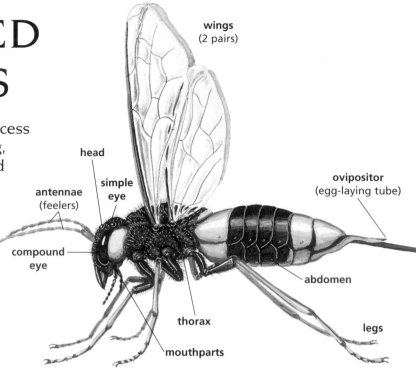

wings
(2 pairs)

head

simple
eye

antennae
(feelers)

ovipositor
(egg-laying tube)

compound
eye

abdomen

thorax

legs

mouthparts

ockroaches are a biological success story. They eat almost anything, including glue, paper, soap, ink and shoe polish. They can even live for three months on just water. Cockroaches have lived on Earth for about 300 million years – since before the dinosaurs. They are just one species in the incredibly successful group called insects.

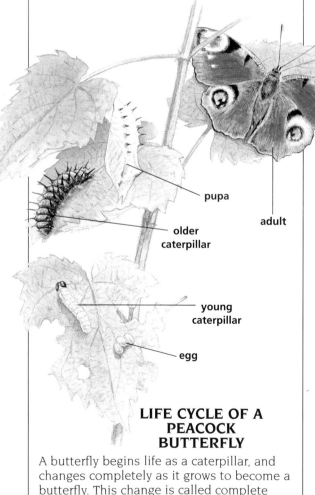

pupa

adult

older
caterpillar

young
caterpillar

egg

**LIFE CYCLE OF A
PEACOCK
BUTTERFLY**

A butterfly begins life as a caterpillar, and changes completely as it grows to become a butterfly. This change is called complete metamorphosis. Other insects look rather like their parents when they hatch. They get bigger and grow wings as they develop. This change is called incomplete metamorphosis.

There are more kinds of insect than of all other forms of life put together. Over 1 million different insects have been named and there may be 10 million more.

Keys to success

Insects have survived so well partly because they are small and breed quickly. And their tough, waterproof, flexible outer skeleton is another important key to their success. The skeleton has allowed insects to dominate almost every habitat except the open sea.

The one drawback of having an outer skeleton is that it does not stretch as an insect grows. So insects have to shed, or moult, their skeleton in order to grow.

Small is good

Most insects are less than 25 millimetres long. Their small size allows insects to live in small spaces and survive on very little food. The smallest insects are fairy flies less than a quarter the size of a pinhead, while the largest insects are not much bigger than a person's hand.

Insect size is limited by the outer skeleton, which can only support light weights, and by the breathing system, which would not work in a large animal.

▲ A typical insect, such as a wasp, has six legs and three parts to its body – the head, the thorax and the abdomen. Most insects also have wings and feelers called antennae on the head.

 key words

- antennae
- insects
- metamorphosis
- moulting
- skeleton
- wings

In a field the size of a football pitch, there are about 200 million insects in the grass and soil.

FISHY TALES

The sailfish can swim at 110 kilometres an hour for short distances – as fast as a cheetah can sprint on land. It is probably the fastest fish in the sea. The sailfish's long, tapering, streamlined body and its powerful tail fin help it to swim fast.

◀ Like the first fishes that crawled out of the water onto the land, mudskippers can breathe in air as well as in water, and crawl over the mud using their stiff, fleshy fins like crutches.

Fishes were the first animals with backbones to live on the Earth. They have existed for nearly 400 million years, and there are more than 25,000 different kinds, or species, today.

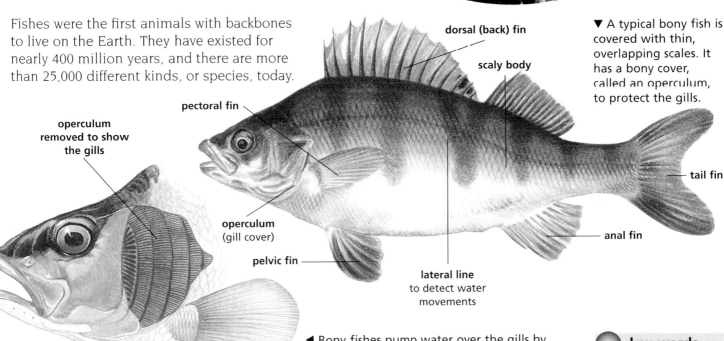

▼ A typical bony fish is covered with thin, overlapping scales. It has a bony cover, called an operculum, to protect the gills.

- dorsal (back) fin
- scaly body
- tail fin
- anal fin
- lateral line to detect water movements
- pelvic fin
- operculum (gill cover)
- pectoral fin
- operculum removed to show the gills

◀ Bony fishes pump water over the gills by opening and closing the mouth and the gill cover. The gills have a large surface area to absorb oxygen from the water.

key words
- backbone
- cartilage
- cold-blooded
- gills
- scales

Scales and gills

The body of a fish is supported by its backbone and protected by a coat of hard, often slippery, scales. Most fishes have gills to take in oxygen from the water. They are cold-blooded, which means that their body temperature changes with the temperature of their surroundings.

Kinds of fish

More than 95 per cent of fishes today are bony fishes. They have jaws, a skeleton made of bone, and a bag of gas called a swim bladder inside their bodies that helps them float and sink.

Cartilaginous fishes, such as sharks and rays, have skeletons made of tough gristle, or cartilage. They do not have a swim bladder. Hagfishes and lampreys are unusual fish groups. They have no jaws, no scales and no proper gills. Their skeleton is made of cartilage.

Fish life cycles

Most fishes lay lots of very small eggs although a few, such as many sharks, give birth to live young. Some eggs float in the sea, while others stick to plants and rocks. Most fishes do not take care of their young.

A DOUBLE LIFE

The male midwife toad hops around for about four weeks with a string of yellow eggs twisted around his back legs. Every so often, he dips the eggs in a pool or a puddle to stop them drying out. When the eggs are ready to hatch, he takes them to a pool and the tadpoles swim away.

Like many other amphibians, midwife toads are caring parents. Amphibians were the first vertebrates (animals with backbones) to live on land, and the first to have true legs, tongues, ears and voice boxes. Most amphibians live a 'double life', partly on the land and partly in the water.

▲ The bright colours of the fire salamander warn predators of its poisonous skin. The poison is even powerful enough to kill small mammals.

Three groups

There are three main groups of amphibians. Salamanders and newts feed on slow-moving animals such as snails, slugs and worms. Most are small and secretive, but giant salamanders grow up to 1.6 metres long, The second group, frogs and toads, are also meat-eaters. They have large, wide mouths to swallow the food that they catch on their long, sticky tongues. The third group, called caecilians, look more like worms than amphibians. They wriggle through the damp soils of tropical forests.

1 day old frog's soft eggs are protected by a jelly-like covering

10 days eggs hatch into tadpoles with a tail but no legs. They breathe through gills

● **key words**
- amphibians
- backbone
- egg
- metamorphosis
- tadpole

▶ A frog has three stages in its life cycle – egg, tadpole and adult frog.

7–13 weeks as tadpole grows, it loses its gills and develops lungs and legs

▲ Caecilians use their heads like garden trowels to dig in the mud for worms, termites and lizards. Adults have a small tentacle on the head to detect chemicals.

Amphibian features

Amphibians do not usually have scales, and their skin is thin, loose-fitting and moist. They usually live in damp places. A few give birth to live young, but most mate and lay their eggs in the water. The eggs hatch into tadpoles, which look very different from the adults. The tadpoles go through a series of changes, called metamorphosis, before becoming adults.

17 weeks frog loses its tail and leaves the water

SCALY SKINS

A cobra rears up and spreads its hood wide. It draws its coils tightly together, ready to lunge forward and sink its poisonous fangs into an enemy or its prey.

Snakes are an unusual group of reptiles with no legs, eyelids or external ears. They are closely related to lizards, which usually have four legs and long tails. Less than a quarter of all snakes use poison (venom) for attack and defence. Other snakes kill by squeezing and suffocating animals tightly in their strong coils.

▲ Turtles may lay up to 150 eggs in a hole they dig on a sandy beach.

Reptile groups

The other main reptile groups, besides snakes and lizards, are turtles and tortoises, and crocodiles and alligators. There were many other reptile groups in the past, including the dinosaurs.

Reptiles have a scaly skin, which stops their bodies from drying out. Unlike amphibians, they can live in dry places. Reptiles are most common in warm places, because their bodies rely on their surroundings for warmth.

Waterproof eggs

One of the most important differences between amphibians and reptiles is that reptiles lay their eggs on land, while amphibians lay their eggs in the water. Even reptiles that live in watery places, such as crocodiles and turtles, lay their eggs on land. Reptile eggs are sealed with a special membrane, the amnion, that stops them drying out. Most reptile eggs have soft, leathery shells, but tortoises, crocodiles and geckos lay eggs with hard shells.

The basilisk lizard can walk – or rather run – on water to escape predators. It relies on its speed, wide feet and fringed toes to stop it sinking below the surface.

▲ A chameleon shoots out its tongue with lightning speed to catch an insect. The sticky tip of its tongue traps the insect.

key words

- amnion
- egg
- reptile
- scaly skin

▼ A crocodile opens its powerful jaws ready to clamp them around the throat of a wildebeest. A crocodile's teeth are brilliant for gripping prey but no good for chewing. So a crocodile swallows its food whole.

MASTERS OF THE SKIES

Swooping silently through the night like a white ghost, a hungry barn owl searches for a meal. Its keen hearing picks up the faint rustling sounds of a mouse scuttling through the leaves. The owl closes in on its victim, its sharp talons sinking into the mouse's warm, furry body.

wing

crown

primary flight feathers

body feathers

bill (beak)

breast

rump

tail

scaly leg

The barn owl is one of nearly 9000 different species (kinds) of birds, which range from the bee-sized hummingbird to the giant ostrich. Birds are different from all other animals in the world because they have feathers. They have wings instead of arms and are the largest, fastest and most powerful flying animals alive today. Birds are also warm-blooded. They can keep their bodies warm no matter how hot or cold it is, so they can live all over the world.

Feathered fliers

Birds are very efficient flying machines. They are very light, partly because many of their bones are hollow. The feathers of a bird give it a smooth, streamlined shape, which helps it to slip easily through the air. The curved shape of the wings helps to lift a bird up into the air, and powerful chest muscles beat the wings up and down.

Flying uses up huge amounts of energy, so birds need to eat plenty of food. They have very efficient lungs to breathe in plenty of oxygen, which they need to 'burn' their food and release energy.

▲ A small bird such as the blue tit has about 3000 feathers, which grow out of pits in the skin, like our hairs. Feathers keep a bird warm, give it shape, colour and pattern and help most birds to fly.

barb

stem

barbules

▼ Frigate birds can soar and glide like vultures but are also fast and agile fliers, like birds of prey. The spectacular red throat sac of the male helps to impress a female during courtship.

▶ A feather is made up of a central stem with side branches (barbs) that are linked together by hooked barbules. If the hooks come apart they can be 'zipped' up again.

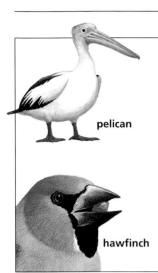

BIRDS' BILLS
The size and shape of a bird's bill depend mainly on what it eats and where it finds its food. The curlew uses its long bill to find worms hidden deep in the mud. The pelican catches fish in its stretchy throat pouch. The flamingo uses its bill as a sieve to strain tiny creatures from the water. The eagle tears the flesh of its prey with its hooked bill. The hawfinch uses its short, strong bill to crack hard seeds.

pelican · hawfinch · curlew · flamingo · eagle

key words
- bird of prey
- courtship
- egg
- feather
- lift
- nests
- warm-blooded

Bird food

Different kinds of bird eat different kinds of food. Some birds are vegetarians, eating fruit, seeds, nuts or leaves. Others eat insects and worms. Many are meat-eaters, catching fish, amphibians, birds and small mammals. The most efficient hunters are the birds of prey, like the eagle and falcon.

ovenbird

weaver bird

Did all the dinosaurs really die out 65 million years ago? Perhaps they didn't. Some scientists think that birds – including the birds in your garden – may be the direct descendants of the dinosaurs.

◀ Ovenbirds and weaver birds build unusual nests. A pair of ovenbirds makes a strong nest the size of a football out of mud and cow dung. Male weaver birds make their nests by weaving together pieces of grass.

▶ Penguins, such as these emperors, have stiff, strong wings, which they use like flippers to swim very fast underwater. Their wings are no use for flying. Other birds that do not fly include ostriches, emus, and kiwis.

Courtship and mating

Male birds are usually more colourful than females and sing or perform daring acrobatics to persuade females to mate with them. After mating, birds lay eggs. They would be too heavy to fly if they carried their young around inside them.

Many baby birds are naked when they hatch from the eggs. They stay safe and warm inside a nest while they grow their feathers. Other birds, such as ducks and geese, hatch out with fluffy feathers. They can run around soon after hatching and feed themselves.

FURRY CREATURES

A group of peccaries shuffles through the forest, unaware of the danger lurking ahead. A jaguar crouches, still and silent, by the side of the track, its spotted coat making it almost invisible in the fading light. At the last moment, the jaguar pounces, grasping a peccary's throat in a suffocating bite.

Cats like the jaguar belong to the same group of animals that we do – mammals. Mammals are generally more intelligent than other animals and are the only animals to have fur or hair. The young of most mammals are born live, although a few mammals lay eggs. Females feed their young on milk produced in special mammary glands on their own bodies.

Worldwide mammals

There are about 4000 different kinds, or species, of mammal. They live all over the world, from icy polar regions to baking deserts and tropical forests. They are able to do this because, like birds, they are warm-blooded. Their body stays at the same high temperature, regardless of the temperature around them.

▲ Seal pups that are born on the ice feed on their mother's very rich milk. This helps them to grow fast and become independent before the ice breaks up.

EGG-LAYING MAMMALS

Monotremes
platypuses and echidnas

LIVE-BEARING MAMMALS

Marsupials
e.g. kangaroos, wallabies, koalas, possums, etc.

kangaroo

platypus

Placental mammals

Insectivores
e.g. hedgehogs, shrews, moles

Primates
lemurs, monkeys, apes and humans

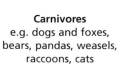
hedgehog

orang-utan

Bats
e.g. fruit bats, mouse-tailed bats, horseshoe bats

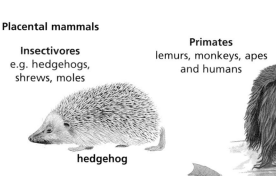
bat

Carnivores
e.g. dogs and foxes, bears, pandas, weasels, raccoons, cats

Edentates
anteaters, sloths, armadillos

giant anteater

weasel

▲ ▶ Living mammals are classified into 21 groups, or orders, based on features that they have in common. The main orders are shown above. The biggest order is the rodents, with 1,700 species.

Mammal young

Mammals are divided into three groups, according to the way their young develop.

Placental mammals give birth to well-developed young. Inside the mother's body, the young are nourished through a special organ called the placenta. Marsupials give birth to tiny young, which finish their development in a pouch on their mother's body. Monotremes (platypuses and echidnas) hatch out of eggs.

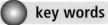
key words
- fur
- mammal
- marsupial
- milk
- monotreme
- placental
- warm-blooded

Sky and sea

The only true mammal fliers are bats. There are hundreds of different bats. They make up one quarter of all mammal species. A bat's wings are made of thin flaps of skin stretched between long finger bones.

Swimming around in the oceans are mammals such as whales, dolphins, sea cows and seals. Their ancestors used to live on land, but they have now made the sea their home. Dolphins, whales and sea cows spend their whole lives in the sea. Seals, sea lions and walruses come out of the sea to breed.

◀ Most mammals have three kinds of teeth: incisors for cutting, canines for gripping and tearing, and molars for grinding up food.

Pinnipedes seals, walruses, sea lions

walrus

Whales dolphins, porpoises, whales

blue whale

Proboscids elephants

elephant

Odd-toed ungulates horses, tapirs, rhinoceroses

rhinoceros

Even-toed ungulates e.g. pigs, camels, deer, giraffes, cattle

red deer

Rodents squirrels, mice, beavers, rats, voles, chipmunks, porcupines

chipmunk

Lagomorphs rabbits, hares, pikas

hare

THE BALANCE OF NATURE

kestrel

vole

grass

◀ Grass, voles and kestrels make up a simple, three-link food chain. The grass is called a producer, because it produces its own food using the Sun's energy. The vole and the kestrel are consumers because they eat ready-made food.

Darting across a city street at night, a red fox narrowly misses being run over by a car. Yet it survives to search through the city's waste bins for scraps of left-over food. Foxes have adapted well to urban life. But many animals have been driven out of their homes by the spread of towns and cities.

Understanding how foxes survive in cities is part of the science of ecology. Ecologists (scientists who study ecology) explore the ways that living things depend on each other for survival. They try to discover the many complicated links between plants, animals and their environment.

Feeding links

One of the ways in which plants and animals are linked together is through their food. Plants make their own food, using energy from sunlight and water from the soil. Animals cannot make their own food – they have to eat plants, or other animals that have already eaten plants. The path that the food follows, through a plant to two or more animals, is called a food chain.

Most animals eat several kinds of food, so they are part of a complicated web of food connections, rather than a simple chain. A food chain usually contains less than six kinds, or species, of animal, but a food web may contain hundreds or thousands.

Living connections

Ecologists recognize that all living things live in particular 'zones' of life. The largest zones are called 'biomes' – these include forests, deserts and grasslands. Each biome is divided into different ecosystems. For example, an oak wood and a pine wood are different ecosystems in a forest biome. Each group, or community, of animals and plants lives in a particular habitat within that ecosystem: perhaps on the forest floor, or high in the canopy of branches.

The individual way of life of a plant or animal is called its 'niche'. A wood ant occupies a niche on the forest floor, while a bird's niche is up in the canopy of branches.

Colonies of ants sometimes make a safe home inside the swollen stems or leaves of special 'ant-plants'. The ants' rubbish provides the plants with extra nutrients.

▶ On the African grasslands, oxpeckers search the skin of large grazing animals, such as this impala, for ticks and bloodsucking flies to eat. Both the oxpecker and the grazing animals gain from their partnership.

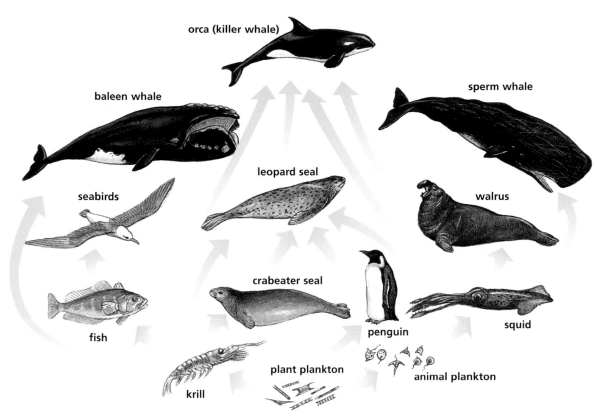

baleen whale
orca (killer whale)
sperm whale
seabirds
leopard seal
walrus
crabeater seal
penguin
squid
fish
krill
plant plankton
animal plankton

◀ This is a simplified food web for an ecosystem in a polar ocean. The producers are plankton, which are like the 'grass' of the sea. A change in just one of the plants or animals in the web will affect all the others.

Wood ants feed on leaf-eating insects. In woodlands where there are no wood ants, the trees lose far more of their leaves to leaf-eating insects than in woodlands where there are wood-ant colonies. So the ants help the woodland trees to thrive. This is one example of the way plants and animals living side by side affect each other in many different ways – not just through food.

Upsetting the balance

There are 6 billion people living on the Earth and the way we live has upset the natural balance of life. We have destroyed or polluted the habitats of many plants and animals and driven some to extinction.

We have changed the climate of the whole world. Understanding ecology can help us to solve the problems we have caused, and to avoid creating new ones.

▼ A map showing the world's biomes. Each biome has a characteristic type of vegetation and wildlife. They are shaped mainly by climate, because this determines where different types of plants can grow.

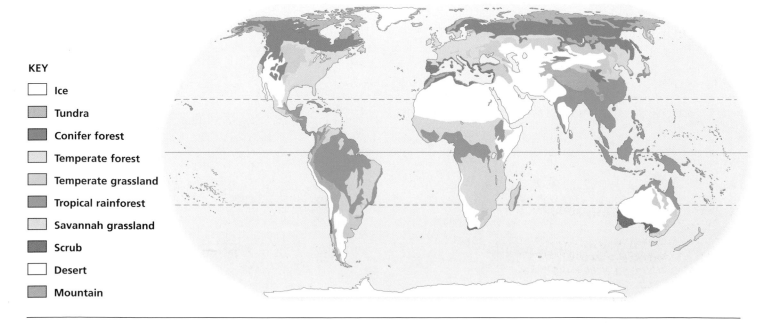

KEY

- Ice
- Tundra
- Conifer forest
- Temperate forest
- Temperate grassland
- Tropical rainforest
- Savannah grassland
- Scrub
- Desert
- Mountain

LIFE AT THE POLES

Every year, a small bird called the Arctic tern makes an amazing journey. It travels over 35,000 kilometres from one end of the world to the other and back again. By making this journey, it escapes from the freezing winter weather in both polar regions.

The North Pole is surrounded by the frozen Arctic Ocean, whereas the South Pole is surrounded by a frozen continent – Antarctica. Few animals, apart from polar bears, can survive on the Arctic ice, but the treeless lands around the Arctic – the tundra – come alive in summer, as animals visit to feed and breed there. In contrast, there is hardly any ice-free land around Antarctica, but the huge variety of life in the oceans during the summer attracts hordes of penguins, whales and seals.

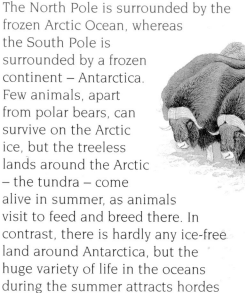

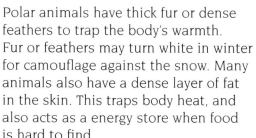

◀ If musk oxen are attacked by wolves, they often form a circle with the young protected in the middle. Musk oxen live on the Arctic tundra all year round.

▲ Low-growing carpets of purple saxifrage cover the Arctic tundra with stunning sheets of colour during the summer months.

Polar plants

Polar plants hug the ground to stay out of the biting winds, and form low, rounded cushions to help trap moisture. In the short summer, plants burst into flower and quickly produce seeds. Many of these seeds survive the winter buried in the soil.

Fur and fat

Polar animals have thick fur or dense feathers to trap the body's warmth. Fur or feathers may turn white in winter for camouflage against the snow. Many animals also have a dense layer of fat in the skin. This traps body heat, and also acts as a energy store when food is hard to find.

key words
- Antarctica
- Arctic
- camouflage
- tundra

▼ The largest bears in the world, polar bears, hunt for seals beneath the Arctic ice. Their big paws have rough, non-slip soles to help them grip slippery snow and ice.

LIFE AMONG THE TREES

High in the branches of a rainforest tree, a poison arrow frog is looking for a place to lay her eggs. In the cup-shaped leaves of a plant called a bromeliad, a pool of rainwater has collected. The mother frog lays her eggs there. Soon the tadpoles hatch and begin to grow, in their own private swimming pool.

Rainforests grow near the Equator, where it is hot and wet all year round. The tree-tops, or canopy, receive year-round rain and sunshine, and the trees are bursting with life. Thousands of different insects, birds and animals live on the leaves, flowers and fruits that the trees provide.

Cooler forests

In other parts of the world, too, forest trees provide food and shelter for the animals and plants that live there. Further away from the Equator, deciduous forests grow in places with warm summers, cool winters and year-round rainfall. Many deciduous trees lose their leaves in winter. In the cool, drier regions across the north of the globe, dark conifer forests grow. The needle-like leaves of the conifers usually stay on the trees all year round.

▼ In the autumn, deciduous forests glow with brilliant red and gold colours as the leaves dry up and fall off the trees. This lets light through to the forest floor and encourages plants to grow, especially in spring.

Surviving the seasons

In both deciduous and coniferous forests life is dominated by the seasons. Spring and summer are times for plants to grow and flower, and for animals to have their young. In the autumn nuts and berries ripen on the trees, and animals feast or store food for the winter. In winter, some birds and mammals migrate, travelling to warmer places to find more food.

◀ A dormouse goes into a deep sleep called hibernation to survive the cold winter months. It uses the fat stored in its body to survive.

● **key words**

- canopy
- coniferous forest
- deciduous forest
- forest floor
- rainforest

At least half of all the animal and plant species in the world live in rainforests.

▼ To get nearer to the light, rainforest plants such as orchids, ferns, mosses and bromeliads perch high on the tree branches.

SEAS OF GRASS

For part of their lives, locusts are solitary insects. But then sometimes, if food runs short, billions of them gather in vast swarms and take to the air. The hungry swarms land on grasslands, and eat all the grass. A large swarm of locusts can eat as much food in a day as 10 elephants or 2500 people.

Grasslands grow in places where it is too dry for forests but too wet for deserts. There are still some natural grasslands left, such as the savannah in Africa, the prairies in North America, the pampas in South America and the steppes in Asia. But in many areas grasslands have been ploughed up by people and used to grow crops.

steppe eagle

hamster

▶ The sharp eyes of the steppe eagle spot prey such as this hamster from high in the air. The eagle swoops in for the kill, using its powerful talons to stun or kill its prey.

Grass and grazers

Grasses are tough plants. Grasslands are home to grazing animals such as antelopes and kangaroos, which chew the grasses almost down to the ground. But most grasses just grow thicker and faster after being eaten. They also grow back well after fires, which are common on grasslands. In dry or cold seasons, grasses die back completely above the ground. Animals may have to migrate long distances to find enough food and water.

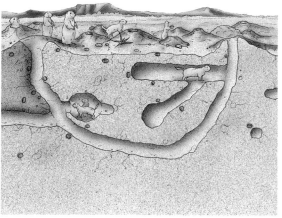

key words

- pampas
- prairie
- savannah
- steppe

◀ Prairie dogs dig tunnels under the North American prairies to escape predators and shelter from hot or cold weather.

Insects

Scurrying around among the grass stems are hordes of tiny insects such as beetles, ants, grasshoppers and caterpillars. Because there are so many of them, insects can eat far more than the big grazers. Many of them, especially termites and dung beetles, play an important role in turning animal dung and the remains of dead plants and animals into rich soil.

◀ These cheetahs have just made a kill on the African savannah. Cheetahs – the fastest land animals on Earth – rely on their speed to catch their prey because they can be seen easily on the open grassland.

LIFE IN THE DESERT

The oversize ears of the African fennec fox can be up to 15 centimetres long. They give off heat rather like a radiator, and so help keep the fox cool. The fox's big ears are also useful for picking up the sounds of its prey when it hunts at night.

Keeping cool and finding food and water are two of the main problems for desert animals. Smaller animals often escape the heat of the day by hiding away beneath rocks or in burrows and coming out in the cool of the night. Most desert animals survive with very little water. Some, such as the kangaroo rat, do not drink at all but get all the moisture they need from their food. Camels store fat in their humps. They can break down this fat to provide them with energy and water.

Desert plants

Desert plants have deep or wide-spreading roots to soak up as much water as possible. Some, such as cacti or pebble plants, store water in swollen stems or leaves. Some plants spend most of their lives as seeds, buried in the desert soil. When it rains, they quickly flower and produce seeds. When the ground dries out again they die, leaving their seeds behind.

key words

- cactus
- camel
- heat
- sand
- water

Shifting sands

Sand is difficult to move across because it shifts and slips under an animal's weight. Camels have wide, cushion-like feet to spread out their weight and stop them sinking. The big hairy paws of the sand cat work in the same way. Sidewinder snakes loop diagonally across the surface of the sand, hardly touching it at all. Lizards called sandfish 'swim' beneath the sand by wriggling their bodies from side to side.

▲To escape the heat of the day, elf owls shelter and nest inside holes in giant cacti. They are the smallest owls in the world.

▼ The dromedary, or Arabian, camel can go for several weeks without water. It can also close its nostrils to keep out drifting sand.

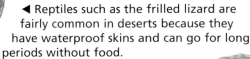

◄ Reptiles such as the frilled lizard are fairly common in deserts because they have waterproof skins and can go for long periods without food.

WETLAND LIFE

▶ A kingfisher flies out of the water after diving to catch a fish in its dagger-like beak. It can make up to 100 dives in one day.

The water spider lives underwater, but it needs to breathe air. So it spins a dome of silk, fixes it to an underwater plant and fills the dome with bubbles of air. The spider leaves its silk bubble when it needs to collect air or catch food, but it always eats its meals at home.

Mosquito larvae also breathe oxygen from the air, using 'snorkels' on the tip of their abdomens. In mangrove swamps, some of the tree roots stick up into the air to take in oxygen. Fishes and tadpoles, however, have gills to take in oxygen from the water, and water plants absorb oxygen from the water over their whole surface. The moving waters of rivers hold more oxygen than the still waters of lakes, marshes and swamps.

Wetland plants

Water is a stronger support for a plant than air, so water plants do not need strong stems or roots. A lot of water plants float near the surface to be near the light they need to make food. Some also use the water to spread their pollen and seeds.

Bogs and marshes often have soils that are poor in some plant nutrients. Unusual meat-eating plants, such as the Venus fly trap, trap insects and other small animals, then digest them to get extra nutrients that are missing from the boggy soil.

Important wetlands

Many animals and birds breed in wetlands because there is plenty of food and shelter. Birds also stop to feed and rest on wetlands during their migration journeys.

Wetlands can help to protect the drier lands around them from storms and floods by soaking up excess water.

Peatlands are wetlands that store tonnes of carbon because they are made of layers of dead plants that do not rot away. If peat bogs are dug up and the carbon dioxide is released, this adds to global warming.

▲ The long, narrow hooves of these lechwe help them to run and leap through swampy ground at great speed. They are also good swimmers

key words

- bog
- mangrove swamp
- marsh
- peat

LIFE BETWEEN THE TIDES

Caught in the strong grip of a starfish, a mussel has little chance of escape. The starfish gradually pulls apart the two halves of the shell, using the many rows of 'tube feet' under its five arms. Then it pushes its stomach out through its mouth and digests the mussel's soft body.

Being attacked by predators is only one of the many problems of living on a seashore. The lives of seashore creatures are dominated by the tides that creep up and down the beach.

As the tide flows in, the shore is covered by floating food. But as it flows out again, creatures are exposed to drying winds, strong sunshine, extreme temperatures and the fresh water in rainfall. Many burrow in the sand or mud or shelter under rocks or seaweed or in rock pools. Some, such as shellfish and barnacles, have tough shells, which help to stop them drying out and protect them from the pounding waves.

Rock-pool life

Rock pools are like tiny, self-contained worlds. The microscopic algae and larger seaweeds in the pool provide food for winkles, limpets and other plant-eaters. The plant-eaters in turn are eaten by meat-eaters such as starfishes, small fishes and

key words
- estuary
- mud
- rock pool
- sand
- scavengers
- seaweed
- tide

▲ When barnacles are covered by seawater, they filter food from the water with their feathery legs. At low tide, barnacles seal their legs inside their shells.

▼ Where rivers meet the sea, they form wide, flat, muddy areas called estuaries. At low tide, wading birds, such as this sandpiper, use their long bills to extract worms, snails and other creatures from the rich mud.

whelks. There are also scavengers such as crabs, that eat dead and decaying plant and animal material.

At low tide a rock pool may quickly heat up or cool down, and the water may become very salty as some of it evaporates away. Plants and animals in the pool have to cope with these rapid changes.

▼ Different plants and animals live in different zones on the shore, according to the amount of time they can survive out of the water.

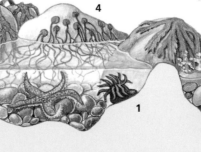

Sea anemones, starfishes and sea urchins (1) live among the seaweeds in the rock pools. These seaweeds include kelp (2), serrated wrack (3) and thong weed (4). Further up the shore live seaweeds such as bladder wrack (5), knotted wrack (6) and spiral wrack (7). Mussels (8), limpets, periwinkles and barnacles (9) have strong shells to protect them. Channelled wrack (10) and lichens (11) flourish on the drier rocks.

LIFE IN THE OCEANS

At the slightest hint of danger, a porcupine fish swallows a lot of water and swells up like a balloon. This makes its sharp spines stick out. Few predators would risk swallowing such a prickly mouthful.

Porcupine fish live on coral reefs, which are home to almost a third of all fish species. These reefs are built up over thousands of years from the skeletons of tiny animals called corals. The coral structures provide a huge variety of places for fishes and other animals to feed, hide and shelter.

Floating food

In areas of the ocean where there are no coral reefs, the basic source of food is the clouds of microscopic floating plants called phytoplankton. These live only in the top 100 metres or so of the oceans, where there is enough light for them to grow. Feeding on the plant plankton are tiny animals called zooplankton.

Plankton cannot swim against the tides and ocean currents, so they drift wherever the water takes them. Larger sea animals, from fishes and birds to huge whales, feed on these drifting masses of plankton.

▶ Many larger sea-dwelling animals live in the open ocean. These include fishes such as the bull shark (1) and tuna (2), sea mammals such as whales, and other creatures such as squid and turtles (3). They often make long journeys in search of food. The much smaller anchovy (4) lives in large shoals near the coasts.

key words
- coral
- photosynthesis
- plankton

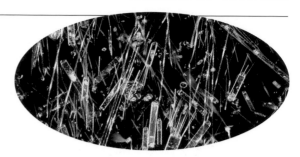

▲ Phytoplankton thrive in nutrient-rich waters where there is plenty of sunlight for photosynthesis. They are most abundant in shallow water.

Life in the deeps

Plants live only in the sunlit surface waters of the oceans, but animals live at all levels. In deep water, animals have to cope with darkness, cold and crushing water pressure. They feed on each other, or on the dead animals, food scraps and droppings that rain down from the sunlit world above.

▲ Coral reefs form in warm, shallow waters. The waters around a reef teem with life. Sea anemones (1), starfishes (2) and crabs (3) live on its surface. Small fishes such as seahorses (4), damsel fishes (5), parrot fishes (6) and clown fishes (7) dart in and out of crevices. Long, thin trumpetfishes (8) hunt for fishes head down, while moray eels (9) hide in the coral to surprise their prey. Manta rays (10) and jellyfishes (11) float above the coral.

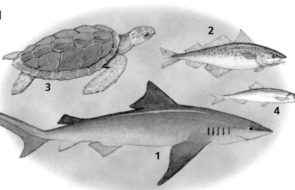

◀ Bottom-dwelling animals often stay in one place and wait for their food to come to them. Some, like the hatchet fish (1) and anglerfish (2), swim along with their large mouths open. The brittle star (3) finds food with its long, thin arms.

SAVING PLANTS AND ANIMALS

By 1980, less than 100 golden lion tamarins survived in the wild. Much of their Brazilian forest home had been cut down, to provide timber and to make way for farms, mines, towns and cities. Tamarins born in zoos have been put back into the wild to try and save the species from extinction.

▲ Tigers, gorillas, giant pandas and thousands of other animal species are in danger of dying out, mainly because their homes in the wild are being destroyed.

Breeding rare animals and plants in captivity is one way to stop them disappearing for ever. But in the long term, they need wild places in which to live if they are to survive. Preserving the habitats of wild

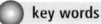

key words

- habitat
- nature reserve
- pollution
- recycling
- zoo

▼ Sea birds that get covered in oil from leaking tankers can sometimes be cleaned up. But we still do not know enough about how the oil from tanker accidents affects the ocean ecosystem.

animals is therefore vitally important. This is often difficult when there are so many people in the world who need places to live and land to farm. But plants and animals are a vital part of our world. Living things help to control the balance of gases, heat and moisture in the atmosphere and the flow of nutrients through the soil. By protecting the Earth's wildlife, we are protecting our own future and the whole planet as well.

Big help

There is a lot that governments and countries can do to conserve plants and animals. They can ban the hunting and collection of rare species. They can stop people selling rare animals or their body parts, such as their horns and skins. They can set up nature reserves to protect vital habitats, and preserve rare species in zoos, botanical gardens and seed banks. And they can pass laws to reduce pollution, which is a major threat to wildlife.

Small help

On a smaller scale, each one of us can make a difference. Scientists help by finding out more about how plants and animals live. The more we know about the natural world, the more we can do to protect it. All of us can help to raise money for conservation work and protest against things that harm living things or their environment. We can recycle waste, reduce pollution from our homes or cars, help to clean up the local environment and encourage wildlife.

GLOSSARY

The glossary gives simple explanations of difficult or specialist words that readers might be unfamiliar with. Words in *italic* have their own glossary entry.

amphibian A *vertebrate* that lives in water and on land, such as a frog or a newt.

arthropod An *invertebrate,* such as an insect or crab, with a segmented body, jointed legs and an *exoskeleton.*

asexual reproduction Reproduction by one parent which does not involve sex cells joining together.

bacteria Microscopic one-celled organisms. Some are useful but a few can cause diseases such as meningitis, tetanus and pneumonia.

biome A very large community of plants and animals living in similar environmental conditions, such as a tropical rainforest, grassland or coral reef.

cell The basic unit of living things.

chromosome A structure made up of *genes*, found in the *nucleus* of a *cell*, which carries genetic information.

cold-blooded An animal such as a fish or an insect whose body temperature changes with that of its surroundings.

DNA (deoxyribonucleic acid) The chemical that makes up *genes.*

ecology The study of the relationship between living things and their environment.

ecosystem A distinct area containing a variety of living things, such as a forest or a lake.

evolution The gradual change in an organism over many generations.

exoskeleton A shell or hard *skeleton* on the outside of an animal's body.

fertilization The fusion of male and female sex cells to make a new living thing.

fossil The remains of a living thing preserved in rock.

genes The parts of a *chromosome* which contain the code for characteristics that are passed on from parent to offspring.

habitat A particular environment, for example the forest floor or a small stream, in which a community of plants and animals lives.

hibernation The way that some animals survive the cold winter months by going into a deep sleep.

invertebrate An animal without a backbone, such as an insect.

mammal A *warm-blooded vertebrate* with fur or hair, that feeds its young on mother's milk.

metamorphosis A major change in an animal's body shape as it grows up.

migration A regular journey made by some animals to reach breeding or feeding areas.

mollusc An *invertebrate* such as a snail, with a soft body that is often protected by a hard shell.

nucleus The control centre of a *cell*, which contains the *DNA.*

photosynthesis The process by which plants make their own food.

pollination The transfer of pollen from the male part of a flower or cone to the female part.

reptile A *cold-blooded vertebrate* with a scaly skin and waterproof eggs.

respiration The process by which food is broken down inside cells to release energy.

sexual reproduction The production of offspring by two parents, in which a male and a female sex cell (in humans, a sperm and an egg cell) join together.

skeleton A strong framework that supports an animal's body.

species A group of the same kind of living things, such as humans or oak trees. Members of a species can breed together.

sperm The male sex cells in animals.

spore A small reproductive or resting structure, usually made of one *cell*, produced by fungi, mosses and ferns.

vertebrate An animal with a backbone.

virus Microscopic organisms, smaller than *bacteria,* that reproduce by infecting living cells. Chickenpox, colds and influenza are all caused by viruses.

warm-blooded An animal such as a bird or a *mammal* that can keep its body at the same warm temperature all the time.

INDEX

Page numbers in **bold** mean that this is where you will find the most information on that subject. If both a heading and a page number are in bold, there is an article with that title. A page number in *italic* means that there is a picture of that subject. There may also be other information about the subject on the same page.

ACKNOWLEDGEMENTS

Key
t = top; c = centre; b = bottom; r = right; l = left;
back = background; fore = foreground.

Artwork
Allington, Sophie: 14 t fore; 33 cl. **Arlott, Norman**:
33 t. **Butler, John**: 41 tl. **D'Achille, Gino**: 7 tl; 19 tr;
25 cr. **Full Steam Ahead**: 45 back; 8 b back.
Gaffney, Michael: 15 t fore; 38 tl. **Gecko Ltd**: 16 r.
Kent, Roger: 10 b; 12 b; 13 br; 12–13 tc back; 19 tr;
20 tr; 39 cr. **Learoyd, Tracey**: 37 b. **Loates, Mick**: 29
c; 44 tl. **Mendez, Simon/Sean Milne/Paul
Richardson/Steve Roberts/Peter Visscher/Michael
Woods**: 34–35 b. **Milne, Sean**: 36 tr; 38; 40 tl; 43 b.
**Milne, Sean/Paul Richardson/Steve Roberts/Peter
Visscher**: 8 bl. **Milne, Sean/Steve Roberts/Peter
Visscher**: 15 t fore; 45. **Ovenden, Denys**: 6 tc.
Oxford Illustrators: 40 c. **Richardson, Paul**: 8 tl,

tr;14 tl, br; 24 tl; 28 tr; 34 tl; 41 br. **Riley, Terry**: 6 b;
7 c; 15 br; 16 bl; 29 cl; 41 bl; 43 tr. **Roberts, Steve**:
23 c, b; 24 br; 26 tl, b; 27 b; 30 tr; 31 tl, tr; 32 tr; 39
tl; 45 tl, tr. **Sanders, Martin**: 32 tr. **Tamblin, Treve**:
14 tl. **Visscher, Peter**: 4 tl; 6 tl; 9 tl, tr; 10 tl; 11 tl,
b; 12–13 tc fore; 16 tl; 18 tl; 18–19 c; 20 l; 22 tl; 28
tl, cl; 29 tl; 30 tl, b; 36 tl; 42 tl; 43 tl. **Woods,
Michael**: 14 bl; 15 t back; 21 b; 25 t; 38 c; 39 tr; 40
tr; 42 tr; 44 b.

Photos
*The publishers would like to thank the following
for permission to use their photographs.*

NHPA: 21 tr; 23 tr (Anthony Bannister). 26 tr (B.
Jones & M. Shimlock); 31 cl (Anthony Bannister);
36 b (Nigel J. Dennis); 38 tr (B. & C. Alexander); 38
b (Andy Rouse); 39 b (John Shaw).

Oxford Scientific Films: 24 tr (Joe McDonald); 14 tr
(G. I. Bernard); 20 bl; 22 tr; 25 b (Densey Clyne
Mantis Wildlife Films); 29 tr (Mark Deeble and
Victoria Stone); 30 br; 31 br (Mark Deeble and
Victoria Stone); 33 br (Kevin Schaefer); 34 tr
(Doug Allan); 42 cr (Carol Farneti Partridge Films
Ltd.); 43 cr (Terry Button); 44 tr (Harold Taylor); 45
bl (Joel Bennett Survival Anglia).

Science Photo Library: 7 bl (Alfred Pasieka); 7 bl
inset (Martin Land); 9 bl (A. B. Dowsett); 10 tr
(Microfield Scientific Ltd.); 11 r (John Mead); 17 tr;
17 br (Nancy Kedersha); 19 br (Philippe
Plailly/Eurelios); 22 b (Eye of Science); 27 tr; 32 b
(Sid Bahrt); 35 t (William Ervin); 40 bl (William
Ervin); 41 tr (C. K. Lorenz).